AND A CHILD
WILL LEAD

Anita M. Constance, S.C.

D1364014

Resurrection Press
An Imprint of
CATHOLIC BOOK PUBLISHING CO.
Totowa • New Jersey

First published in September 2003 by
Catholic Book Publishing/Resurrection Press
77 West End Road
Totowa, NJ 07512

Cover photo by Anne Cousineau

Cover design by Beth DeNapoli

Printed in the United States

1 2 3 4 5 6 7 8 9

To my niece
Lisa Michele
and
my nephews
Kyle, Tyler and Johnathan

Contents

The wolf shall live with the lamb,
   the leopard shall lie down with the kid.
the calf and the lion and the fatling
     together,
  and a little child shall lead them.

—Isaiah 11:6

Foreword

In every adult there lurks a child—an eternal child, something that is always becoming, is never completed, and calls for unceasing care, attention, and education. That is the part of the human personality which wants to develop and become whole. (C. G. Jung)

THESE words of Carl Jung describe what we refer to today, in therapy, as the work of *healing the inner child*. The anguish that is experienced in life as depression is often associated with unresolved issues that are rooted in childhood.

It is not uncommon to hear clients report their earliest memory in these words: "I'm two years old sitting in my high-chair looking at my mother." . . . "I feel three years old and I'm crying." . . . "I see my father with his belt, yelling at me; maybe I'm six." . . . "I'm in the fifth grade and the teacher is angry and the whole class is laughing." . . . "I'm not able to remember anything before twelve years of age."

The adult client is seeking healing from a lifelong struggle with depression, nameless dread, rejection and misplaced guilt. In therapy, the child is finally free to express these feelings, in order to deal with the anguish that has held the adult client captive. The journey is often long but also gracefilled.

Anita Constance has uniquely captured the heart of Jung in *And a Child Will Lead*. Selecting the children of scripture, she helps us focus on inner healing—the healing of our *child within*—healing from the applause of others to self-affirmation, from rejection to self-esteem, from unforgiveness to acceptance, from dread to peace, from depression to hope, from fear to freedom, and from grasping to grace. The story of each child names the gift that the adult seeks and presents the grace needed for transformation through the healing of Jesus Christ. It is the eternal *child*, the *child within*, who calls for our unceasing care, attention and education—the essentials for our wholeness. *And a Child Will Lead* provides the setting for all of us to find the healing presence of Christ.

Dr. Catherine Morrisett, S.C.

♰ Introduction ♰

I CANNOT remember my own birth, but I would like to think of it as my first "yes" to God. I would like to think that I *will-ingly* cooperated with God and truly participated in my own birth by that "yes." If this is so, our participation in God's will, our "yes" from birth into eternity, is always creative—filled with life, no matter the experience.

I believe that creation is the expression of the maternity of God. We are part of creation, yet in a way unique among all others. The image and likeness of God have graced us. We were born of God, formed into divine life; but we were also born into God, into the inexhaustible Mystery of Love. Our God of love believed in us then, now and into eternity. We continue to carry our divinity even when we have lost the awareness of this gift of greatness that we are.

As the expression and reflection of our Creator, we have the responsibility to become co-creators with God, co-creators of our very selves—this is our daily "yes." It is not a burden but a gift—the gift of freedom that leads us over and over again to new life, to fullness of life. *And a Child Will Lead* is an opportunity to continue our own creation with and in God. It is an opportunity to look within to find those places in need of healing—those places that were filled with integrity and wholeness at our conception, but became wounded or scarred by persons and experiences through the years.

How do we do this? We must let go—let ourselves go into the heart of God—tumble down into the Mystery of God within us. It is there that we find compassion and healing. We let God be God for us and surrender ourselves to mercy, compassion and healing love. Commitment is the work of surrender. It is Jesus

Christ, the Son of God and our Brother, who shows us the way. Jesus is surrender itself; he is commitment; he is endless hope and glorious fulfillment. Jesus assures us, "Did I not tell you that if you believed, you would see the glory of God?" (Jn 11:40). We are the glory of God—thanks to God! In the light of Christ, we will see our brokenness and our faults but also our gifts. In Christ we will come to believe that we truly are the glory of God. In a sense our healing is a return to our beginnings, yet it is a transformation into glory—God's glory—the whole and holy persons of God's original intention.

To be faithful to the process, we must depend upon God's grace. We must lean into this grace because grace is for the long haul. It will never fail us; grace keeps us faithful in the face of our limitations. We also need a vision that penetrates through those places in need of healing as with the eyes of God—a graced vision. When we see our life experiences through the eyes of grace, we know that what we touch and what touches us are opportunities for the blessing of God. God invites us to use all things, all experiences—past, present and future—for our healing. Nothing, no circumstance or event, is void of God's presence no matter how difficult or painful it seems. We carry God with us into every experience of the day. Healing follows this act of faith; we stand on the threshold of resurrection and new life each time we enter into those moments. What is difficult for us is also our grace, the place of our healing—the doorway to the transformations for which we long.

And a Child Will Lead is an invitation to accept the struggle we may meet along the way and to engage it. Despite our fears, we will not be destroyed. Our fears, failures and limitations are human vessels waiting to be filled with new life. Jesus saves us from the depth of our fears and the death of our fears. When we can do nothing, God can do everything. It is precisely our powerlessness, the powerlessness of our *child within,* that opens the way to Jesus who is healing and new life. The thing we fear most can become the *wholing* of our strength—there, discouragement becomes hope and power is commitment.

We must remember Jesus. We must remember that not one drop of the blood he shed is without meaning. No tear falls from our eyes without leaving us cleansed. No failure, no betrayal is so great that Jesus will not reach down and lift us into his healing arms. Resurrection, new life and healing happen each time we hand ourselves over to him—each time we surrender that piece of ourselves we feared to hold out to the Light of Christ. Healing happens even in the quiet and hesitant expression of our desire for healing. Jesus asks only that we come to him, nothing else: "Come to me, all you that are weary and are carrying heavy burdens, and I will give you rest" (Mt 11:28). There in his presence, we experience the peace of Christ—inner peace and security— that frees us to accept life as it is and to treat others with forgiveness, gentleness and compassion. We must greet this *child within* us with open hands and hearts, and offer him or her a new beginning. The hope of healing is the hospitality we offer our inner selves, because our faith has faced Christ who longs to heal us.

Jesus performed miracles that inspired some to have faith in him and others to fear him. These pages speak of the miracles in which children received healing and life through faith in Jesus Christ. It can be a parent who intercedes on the child's behalf, or the adult child, himself or herself, or the experience of a child's generosity as an instrument of grace. But in all, it is faith that touches, pleads, cries out to the heart of Jesus—the heart of God. It is faith that keeps the pray-er faithful. It is faith that makes all the difference. Faith in miracles is really faith in the power of love.

Part One of this book lays the foundation of this process toward healing: Why *Go Within?* What will we find? Will we have the strength to engage it?—Why *Jesus?* Is this Son of God truly our brother? How can I identify with him?—Why *Childhood?* Isn't this regression or weakness? Am I wasting my time with the past?

Part Two of *And a Child Will Lead* offers reflections on the gospel, prayer and guided meditations to remind us that Jesus heals. This strengthens our hope in him today and keeps us faithful to the process. Each reflection is followed by a Faith-Word: words we struggle to say, acts of faith amid our fears and uncertainties; a Heart-Word: spoken boldly from the truth within our hearts; and God's Word: reflections of God's loving care for us. These statements of belief can be prayed individually over several days, allowing the hope and courage of each "word" to prepare the holy ground within us for the guided meditation that follows. This process is not meant to be rushed and may be helpful to repeat after the meditation, as well.

The Prayer Services and Rituals found at the end of this book are further invitations to acknowledge and explore the rich gift of self that God intended for each of us. These may be prayed with a group or reflected upon in personal prayer.

This journey to healing and wholeness is a lifetime journey, a Christian journey. It began with Abraham, our father in faith, who left everything he knew for a place known only by the promise of God. We continue, in his spirit, to set out for a land we fear may never be reached—our healing—but still a destination we, too, know in the promise of God. We cross the desert of our doubts with Moses, led by our own cloud of unknowing, fired with God's promise in Jesus Christ.

Perhaps you have visited this promised land before but continued on. Perhaps you would like to return to that mystery of God within and remain there. Perhaps you are just setting out, seeking the fullness of life and the healing for which you have longed. Come to the quiet place of your true self where all is well, where wellness and peace await you. Come in the spirit of a retreat—at home or away. It is my hope that these pages will support and nourish you on your journey.

Anita M. Constance, S.C.

A Meditation of Hope

In the beginning . . . *there was GOD.*

In the moment of conception's gift . . . *there was GOD.*

In the darkness of my mother's womb . . . *there was GOD.*

In the stirrings of growth within and outside . . . *there was GOD.*

In my simplest of movements . . .*there was GOD.*

In the gentle flowing that cradled my being . . . *there was GOD.*

In the cord of life that nurtured my needs . . . *there was GOD.*

In my turning toward the tunnel of birth . . . *there was GOD.*

In the helping forth of my mother's struggle . . . *there was GOD.*

In my breathing in of redemptive-life . . . *there was GOD.*

In my breathing out of redeeming-love . . .*there was GOD.*

PART ONE

– 1 –

Going Within

I praise you, O God,
for calling me to the center
of all things—
to the center of you—
to the center of me
that is you.

THERE is a story . . .

When God finished making the world, God wanted to leave behind for human beings a piece of divinity—God's own divinity—a spark of that essence, a promise to us of what we could become, with effort. God looked for a place to hide this divinity because, God explained, what we could find too easily would never be valued by us.

"Then you must hide the Godhead on the highest mountain peak," said one councilor.

"Not there," said God, "for humans are adventurous creatures and they will soon enough learn to climb the highest mountain peaks."

"Hide it then, O Great One, in the depths of the earth!"

"I think not," said God, "for my people will one day discover that they can dig into the deepest parts of the earth."

"In the middle of the ocean then, O King?"

With shaking head God replied, "I have given each person a brain, you see, and one day they will learn to build ships and cross the mightiest of oceans."

"Where then, my God?" cried the councilor.

God smiled. "I'll hide it in the one place that they will hardly think to look. I'll hide it deep inside their hearts. It will be my surprise—my gift!"

Was God playing a trick on us? Setting up a game of sorts? A challenge impossible to meet? No, God wants us to seek *and* to find. *Going within* is opening the door to God. It is the response we make to God's invitation to pay attention to our hearts. Why is this so important? How do we know that our *going within* will bring us to God? How do we know that we will meet Jesus in the midst of our hopes, fears, disappointments and dreams? William Wordsworth, in his *Ode on Intimations of Immortality*, writes: "Trailing clouds of glory, we come from God who is our home."

At Baptism, we were baptized into Jesus Christ, into the very Son of God. In chapter 12 of his first letter to the Corinthians, St. Paul tells us that we are the *body* of Christ. Couldn't we say then that it is within our own bodies that we meet the person of Jesus? He resides there as both our life force and our healing God. St. Paul also tells us that we are temples of the Holy Spirit—the Spirit who fulfilled the promise of Jesus to be with us all days. Why would we not, then, enter this temple of God—our bodies—to pray, to seek and to find? To ask for our heart's desires and to satisfy our heart's longings? St. John of the Cross prayed, "O thou Soul, most beautiful of creatures who longest to know where thy beloved is, thou art thyself that very tabernacle where [he] dwells." We are sacred space; we are holy ground. We are the place where good things happen each time we enter the presence of God-within.

Jesus told us that he is the Way, the Truth and the Life (Jn 14:6). When we *go within,* we enter the place of that truth. We touch our true selves where God dwells at peace and at one with us. But, oftentimes, layers of loss and wounded emotions cover our wholeness and cloud the peace that rests at the center of our hearts. Still, we are reminded of the loving presence that sustains and strengthens us—God is close to the brokenhearted, and those who are crushed in spirit are saved (Ps 34:19). Nothing can separate us from the love of Christ! Then what should we do? We must go to those broken places and the moments that crushed our hearts, and meet the grace God offers. Scripture assures us that by [his] wounds we are healed (Is 53:5). St. John of the Cross reminds us: "Out of our scars, God creates our beauty." So it is the wounds of the whip that become the place of our healing.

God is with us! God is in us! *Going within* answers the call to come home, to visit the dwelling place of God and reconnect with what is loved. It is an invitation to attend to our unfinished business; heal the memories that abide in the aches and pains of the past; dress "the wounds of the whip" with our attention and the loving presence of God.

With what do we return home? With hope. Who will make this journey with us? Jesus. Why should we set out on this path? It is necessary. In the words of Karl Rahner: "The treasury of the past is the freedom of the future" *(The Great Church Year).* Despite our helplessness, we experience hopefulness. We go in prayer, for prayer unveils our desire for God. Our true self lies in the love and mercy of God, and God is determined to hear us! Perhaps the question we must ask ourselves as we begin this journey is, "Can I see myself from God's point of view?" Can I accept that God loves me simply because "I am," knowing that accomplishments are not necessary for my value? Can I believe, or at best hope, that the life of Christ within me has been waiting to gift me with his healing touch?

Fear can cause us to run away from our questions; with faith, we stop running. By *going within,* we not only face our questions, we run toward them and remain with them. This is the first step on the road to healing. Yes, it requires courage because we are entering the heart of Mystery but the Mystery is God. God does not intend to frighten us but to fulfill us. With God, we do not need the answers. Instead, we receive the fullness of God in all the ways we are in need. With mystery, all the pieces cannot be named; we see only in part. But in the Mystery of God, God can name them all and will heal them all in Jesus.

It is not so much a matter of what has happened to us, or what someone has done to us that adds the layers of loss that cover our true self. It is more a matter of losing touch with those experiences and their meaning for us. It is our life's task to revisit those experiences, again and again, until we have uncovered fully our true self. We must go through those layers of loss and pain to encounter our God who lives within us and desires to be made manifest fully through us.

Going within is a path to love—love of ourselves. This is not a self-satisfying, self-seeking path but a path to the God of love who finds us lovable. In the first letter of Paul to the Corinthians, Chapter 13, we read that we can have all knowledge but if we do not have love, we are nothing. In many ways the saying is true—

knowledge is not everything. We can know all the details of our past, far back into childhood, but knowing does not create change. We must first *go within* to create kinship, kinship with ourselves. There we listen to the stories of our lives, paying attention to our feelings and addressing old wounds. Then we will find that what was once vulnerable has become venerable. Yes, *going within* is a path to love.

Jesus meets us where we are as we make this journey. He walks with us as we touch the place of our truth. We can begin this journey sooner or later, that does not matter to God. God is faithful and fully present in the journey, whenever and wherever the journey may lead. We were not made in pieces, yet God gives us a lifetime to discover our wholeness. Can we trust that no matter what we meet along the way, there is a sustaining Truth that will support us—a source of courage, perseverance, even long-suffering? Yes! God's plan for us is life, not death; hope, not despair; peace, not disaster. God's plan is that we be holy and whole. This is not wishful thinking. This is God's intention for us.

> Deep within us all is an amazing sanctuary of the soul,
> a holy place, a Divine Center, a speaking Voice, to
> which we may continuously return. Eternity is at our
> hearts, pressing upon our time-torn lives, warming us
> with intimations of an astounding destiny, calling us
> home unto itself.   (Meister Eckhart)

– 2 –

Jesus . . . Son of God and Our Brother

Little lamb, who made thee?
Who made me?
Lamb of God,
Sheep and Shepherd—
You sit at the door.
You are the door—
the gate
the way through
to my God.
Transparency of grace.

JESUS is the Way, the Truth and the Life for the *child within*. Throughout the gospels, we see how comfortable Jesus was with children. He gathered them to himself, enjoyed their presence, mentioned them in his stories and blessed them, again and again. With confidence, we give our *child within* to Jesus for healing because he truly cares. Yet even more . . . Jesus understands us because he is one of us. The gospel according to John announces this news of great joy: And the

21

Word became flesh! The Son of God is one of us in Jesus Christ. This flesh was no costume for God, no disguise to trick us into thinking that our wildest dream had come true. The Word became flesh not to fool us but to entice and beckon us further into Mystery.

The Word of God became flesh! The Word spoken from the mouth of God became a human transubstantiation of God's very self. Through Baptism, Jesus is our heart, and we are his body. What does all this mean? How are we affected by this truth? What responsibility accompanies this reality? Karl Rahner says, "There is only one thing we are not to do: will to be less than brothers and sisters of the eternal Word of the Father who became flesh" *(The Great Church Year)*.

To appreciate this we must break down any barriers that prevent us from calling Jesus our brother . . . any barriers that keep us from believing that Jesus was like us in all things, except sin. Jesus was like us and is for us, yet Jesus is more . . . Jesus is what we are called to become. Jesus is the core of our reality, the heart—the center of all that makes us human:

> Jesus . . .
> bone of my bone, flesh of my flesh.
> heart at the center of my heart.
> voice within my voice.
> word of all my words.
> holy nearness of my presence.
> source of my origin.
> end of my goals.
> power of my strength.
> humility of my weakness.
> fullness of my satisfaction.
> desire of all my dreams.

sense of my knowing.
mystery of my unknowing.
anticipation of my longing.
future of my hope.
vision of all my seeing.

We hold eternity even closer than the palm of our hands. We, ourselves, hold eternity and divinity in our very bodies, our very being. Because of Jesus, we are the chalice, the cup, the bowl of divine fullness. Because of Jesus, we hold heaven on this earth. Because of Jesus, we are transformed into the divine—held in human flesh. Because of Jesus, we outweigh silver and gold. Because of Jesus, we breathe in divinity to breathe forth our humanity. Because of Jesus, we will one day breathe out this humanity into the Mystery of eternity.

God tells us in scripture:

> For as the rain and the snow come down from heaven,
>   and do not return there until they have watered the
>   earth,
> making it bring forth and sprout,
>   giving seed to the sower and bread to the eater,
> so shall my word be that goes out from my mouth;
>   it shall not return to me empty,
> but it shall accomplish that which I purpose,
>   and succeed in the thing for which I sent it.

(Is 55:10-11)

We are the recipients of the fullness of God in Jesus, the Word. We are the achievement of Jesus' loving obedience to his ABBA. Our healing, our salvation, our wholeness is God's good pleasure.

Knowing all this, we now turn to Jesus, the child. Our *child within* can find comfort, hope and healing in this child. He has much to teach us although there is so little in scripture about this stage of his life. Since Jesus was conceived within a woman by the power of the Holy Spirit, perhaps we can conjecture certain things because of the human life we share with him . . .

In the gospel according to Luke (1:26-38), we read the story of the Annunciation. Mary said "yes" to the mystery of motherhood for the Son of God. Could we not say that Jesus was conceived at the moment of that "yes"? Then the beginning of his life took place within an event of affirmation, a "yes" event. Mary's faith-response confirmed God's will for her and at the same time affirmed Jesus, the life within her womb. Surely Mary's acceptance of mystery and new life filled her being. The very cells of her body communicated to Jesus a love, an acceptance and a faith that would form and inform his entire life. Certainly the gamut of her emotions touched the embryonic beginnings of Jesus with wonder and joy. Jesus would grow and come to know that wonder and joy as he uncovered the depths of the mystery—how fully he possessed and was possessed by God.

Yes, Mary wonders but she never doubts the gift. Her wholehearted "yes" blessed the world and us with the gift of salvation. As God was fully present at the moment of the conception of Jesus, God was fully present at the moment of our conception. Whether intended or unintended, our conception was attended by Love itself—a Love we can depend upon today. If we were not affirmed by our parents, perhaps the "yes" for each of us needs to be spoken now in our adult years . . . a "yes" that comes from our own hearts, our own truth—the place within where God has long dwelled and to which Jesus leads us.

What is your faith-response to the gift of God—God's creation of you?

In Luke 1:39-56, we witness Mary's visit with her cousin Elizabeth; she went quickly to her cousin's side. How much they must have shared, having both been entrusted with the great task of mothering. When they met, Mary and Elizabeth praised God who was active in their lives. They knew that the conceptions of Jesus and John were both extraordinary. Besides the comfort these cousins could bring to one another, Mary and Elizabeth shared the mystery that was growing inside their wombs—the mystery of God creating life when least expected. Together they would begin to unwrap the gift.

In salvation history, the child of one would prepare the way for the child of the other. The clear, sheer joy of this was expressed as John leapt in the womb of his mother. I believe we could say that Jesus learned the importance of family and loving relationships through this communication of child to Child. For Jesus, the importance of family would lead to a community of believers. For John, it would bless his heart with a humility that acknowledged his cousin as the Lord.

Through Jesus, faith teaches life. The Mystery of God touches our lives in unexpected ways each day, creating new life in unexpected ways. Jesus can bring love to our relationships through his healing grace. He can help us recognize new persons to call "family"—people who nurture us and find joy in us. We, too, can share the mysteries of our lives with another. Through Mary, the fullness of Life embraced humankind. That Life, who is Jesus, continues to embrace us today.

With whom do you seek to share and unwrap the mysteries of your life?

The birth of Jesus is told simply, yet grandly, in Luke 2:1-20. Amid angels, stars and shepherds, our Savior Jesus is born. It was a humble birth. He was dressed in swaddling clothes and laid in a manger upon straw. The host of humanity was born homeless. The bread of heaven slept upon the feed of animals. And the invited guests were shepherds from the surrounding fields. Yes, God reveals to the "little ones" the mysteries of the kingdom!

Today the angels say to us, "Do not be afraid; for see—I am bringing you good news of great joy for all the people: to you is born this day . . . a Savior" (Lk 2:10-11). Jesus is the Savior who makes us whole. Like us, he knew the birth pains of his mother as he slowly turned in her womb, preparing to gift our earth with the presence of God. His arrival was heralded by few, yet he would lead us to union with God and all others. Truly a sign of contradiction, we find in the powerlessness of an infant the strength of one who brings peace.

All that Jesus experienced had a purpose on the journey to salvation. We, too, have a purpose in life. All things have a purpose—even a star served to lead the shepherds and wise men to Jesus. But true wisdom tells us that each of us must be someone before we can do anything. We must believe in ourselves before we can give ourselves away to the world. Today is our day of salvation! Each day is. Our journey is rich in experience and meaning. What we perceive as powerlessness can find hope and peace in the birth of Jesus. The signs of contradiction that have made their home in our hearts can become places of inner wisdom and knowing. In Jesus, we will discover the treasure of ourselves and the meaning of our lives. There we will become the star that burns in the night and leads others to Jesus.

What helps you discover the meaning of your life?

At the circumcision and dedication of Jesus, according to Luke 2:21-38, we meet two elderly believers in the kingdom of God—Simeon and Anna. Jesus, as first-born male, was brought to the temple. He experienced the Jewish ritual of consecration to God in the presence of two keepers of the "promise." Through this ritual, Jesus became a child of God—one with God's chosen people in whom salvation would be achieved.

As an infant, did Jesus understand all that happened that day? All that was announced by Simeon? All that was praised by Anna? At our Baptism, did we understand the full grace and meaning of that sacrament? No, but we did understand the love of arms that cradled us. We did feel the warmth of smiles upon us. We did experience contentment in the exchange of joy that was shared. *And* we became heirs of God's promise too—salvation to be achieved in faith, hope and love; new life given to us through water and the Spirit.

As Simeon and Anna gathered around him, Jesus met his wisdom figures—the mentors of his fledgling faith. Wisdom figures are often those who know us better than we know ourselves, those who believe that we make a difference in life and show us why we do. Grandparents take that role for some of us or sometimes teachers. If this was not our experience within our families or during our school years, hopefully some person or persons stepped into our lives with the love and affirmation we longed for and needed. Love and affirmation are essential birthrights. We are *entitled*, in the most sacred sense of the word, to be loved. This experience of Jesus—the day he was dedicated in the temple, the day he was embraced by the faith of Simeon and Anna—can bring to mind all those who believed in us through the years.

Who are your wisdom figures, your mentors in the faith?

It is only when Jesus is twelve years old that we hear his first words, found in Luke 2:41-50. These are spoken in response to the anxiety of his parents: "Why were you searching for me?" He questioned. "Did you not know that I must be in my Father's house?" (Lk 2:49). In other words, Jesus' life was to be about his ABBA, to live fully in the presence of God and to dwell in union with the will of God.

This was a most important moment in his life. It was no longer necessary for someone else to speak for Jesus, telling who he was: not angels or wise men, not Mary or Elizabeth, not Simeon or Anna. Jesus spoke for himself! But Mary and Joseph did not understand their son. They did not comprehend the full reality of his words. His place in the temple, his union with God, took precedence over his relationship with them.

The same is true for us. The divine life dwelling within us, the temple of God that we are, is what we are about. What is our deeply rooted identity? We are sons and daughters of God! Once we can claim this for ourselves, we, too, will be free to live fully our true reality. The incarnation is the divine embrace of human limitation. The embrace of God graces our humanity. Actually, the embrace itself is our humanity in Jesus Christ. Human life, then, is a height to be reached, not an excuse to fall short. Jesus, the boy of twelve years, was beginning to understand this. He was beginning to understand who he was. This boy, Jesus, is our brother! And . . .

> to all who received him,
> who believed in his name,
> he gave power to become children of God. . . .
> From his fullness we have all received.
>
> (Jn 1:12, 16)

*Recall the moment in which you were able to speak your
own truth . . .
when you realized your special identity in God.*

– 3 –

 Children of God

O embrace of the cross,
in whose arms I know
my healing—
Let me not forget
the embrace of flesh
that first gathered me,
held me, touched me,
loved me.

A S we matured physically and mentally, we could not wait
to put away childish things. Initially, it took the form of
being "grown up" like Mom and Dad—helping them with
chores around the house, dressing up, imitating them.
Growing into our teen years, we looked ahead; adulthood
could not come fast enough. The old family photos, the toys
of our youth, all became embarrassments. Independence was
budding within us and we ached for the freedom of adulthood
to blossom it forth. We thought we knew all the answers and
that we could conquer the world. How we longed to be adults!
But we open the scriptures and find Jesus saying: " . . . unless
you change and become like little children you will never enter

the kingdom of heaven" (Mt 18:3). What is going on here? We worked hard at growing up and becoming independent. Are we supposed to give that up now? Are we supposed to revert to a role of dependency?

Yes and no. St. Paul tells us:

> For you did not receive a spirit of slavery to fall back into fear, but you have received a spirit of adoption. When we cry, "Abba! Father!" it is that very Spirit bearing witness with our spirit that we are children of God. (Rm 8:15-16)

There is nothing weak about being a child of God. There is nothing immature. In truth, it is a challenge. This is precisely what Jesus tells us when he gathers children to himself, embraces and blesses them. By his words and actions, Jesus assures us that children are significant. But even more, he advises us to pay attention to them and to imitate them, become like them. Jesus makes it clear that no matter how old we are, if we want to have a place in the kingdom of heaven, we must become like children.

Nicodemus felt the challenge of this, as well: "How can anyone be born after having grown old? Can one enter a second time into the mother's womb and be born?" (Jn 3:4). No, that would be impossible. To believe that this is what Jesus intended would be naïve. Jesus lifts Nicodemus out of the enclosure of his thinking and speaks of a rebirth by water and the Spirit—the Holy Spirit of God. Jesus breaks through the barriers of human limitation and announces a greater, fuller reality. It is through Baptism that we are born again. It is through Baptism that we become children—children of God—and continue in that relationship forever. Should this threaten our sense of self as adults? No, because this relationship is an invitation to a courageous life of ever deepening faith, joy, hope, healing and peace. When Jesus, our brother, invites us to become children, he empowers us, not diminishes us.

For Jesus, it is not a question of status that makes a person great and worthy of the kingdom; it is just the opposite. Dependence and simplicity carve out and develop our capacity for the fullness of life that he promised. The complete dependence, joyful spontaneity, natural receptivity and simple wonder of a child serve to remind us of how we must be with God. We, the adult children of God, can experience such complete dependence as creative because it is the basis of our courage and inner freedom.

> If children, then heirs,
>
> heirs of God and joint heirs with Christ.
>
> (Rm 8:17)

What is our inheritance as co-heirs with Christ? We can now confront our fears, and tend to our *child within*, confident in God who is dependable. We can trust spontaneity because it is God's grace. We can allow the gift of receptivity to be fulfilled, and witness our wonder as it pursues the adventure of eternal life. We can call out to the One who was there before we were born. The One who ushered us from thought into being. The One through whom all things were created—the Word, Jesus. We can invite Jesus into the secret places where our *child within* continues to fear and to doubt. Jesus wants us to ask, to pray:

> Healing God, touch us at our point
> of anguish this day.
> That place which is known only to you.
> That place that can be touched only by you.
> No one else could find that place
> and know it to be so.

Even we are unsure of the broken places
and wounded spaces within.
Healing God, touch us at our point
of anguish this day.
Anoint those secret scarrings
with the sacred oil of reverence
for what is yet unhealed.
May our struggles yield to that touch
and give way to your healing. Amen.

Having seen the treasure that lies within us . . .
Having found Jesus to be our faithful companion
and loving brother . . .
Having affirmed the value of the children of God . . .

with confidence,

we begin

the journey of healing . . .

PART TWO

– 4 –

From Applause to Affirmation

Angel of God, my guardian dear,
hold fear from my life.
Bridle its reins that it may not
reign in my heart and establish
a kingdom that walls out
life and possibility.
Keep me defenseless against grace.
Unseal the doors I have closed
so that God may catch me unaware,
for at times it is surprise,
and only surprise,
that can throw open
the doors of my heart.

Take some time to read and ponder . . . John 4:46-53

THE PLACE OF HEALING

"Sir, come down before my little boy dies!" (Jn 4:49).

THE court official in this gospel story was frantic about the health and well-being of his son. A fever roared through the boy's body and now he lay in the grip of death. This father was a man of position and authority; most likely he had access to every avenue of conventional healing. Unsuccessful in providing a cure for his son, it no longer mattered that he was an outsider to Jewish blood and belief; desperation drove him to Jesus.

But what was the fever that burned so fiercely within his boy? What drove the flame of illness so wildly that it was destroying his son's body?

Could he have been challenged from early on to present himself as the son of a public figure? To live up to the expectations of others by acting as he felt he should, rather than with the spontaneity and simplicity of childhood? Did he experience, unknowingly, a tension within or a separation from the true child he was?

When this happens in life we feel the pressure of perfection. We are ruled by the power to please, and that can rise to fever pitch, wounding the heart of our *child within*. This is not the perfection that Jesus encourages us to seek, "Be perfect, therefore, as your heavenly Father is perfect" (Mt 5:48). That perfection would make us whole, integrated persons. The unhealthy pursuit of perfection is a driving and destructive force. It gains a momentum that can engulf us and snuff out the light of our uniqueness, keeping us far from the intentions of Jesus. This perfection reaches deep into the spirit and roots itself in a childhood motivated to please, to achieve, to excel. Sadly, it is both an illusion and forever elusive. We begin to look at ourselves from the outside in, losing sight of our true self.

As we grow up, this fire of perfection grows out of control and pushes us off course, driving us in ways we no longer understand. It sends us down paths we should not choose; yet we go and still it drives us. It is fanned to such a fury that it burns us in the process; worry and useless anxiety are the allies of this desperate need to succeed and to please.

If we are plagued by this fire of perfection and realize its fever pitch, we long to be healed. Like the father, frantic, we cry out to Jesus, "Come, before my *child* dies!" Yes, we too can make our way to Jesus in faith. Jesus sees that faith, is touched by our hope in him and will not deny our plea. It may take a long time for the fire to die down and the flames to extinguish, but faith and effort are both the beginning and the cure. In the court official's heart, faith and hope crossed the lines of all division and the bridge to healing was built. "Go home, your son will live!" Jesus told him. With that he believed, and with expectation in his heart, he went on his way. Before he arrived home, the gospel tells us that his servants met him with the news that his boy was alive. The child's fever had broken the moment Jesus spoke his words of compassionate assurance,

"Go home, your son will live!" These words of Jesus are meant for our *child within*. The fever of perfection will cool for us as well. With expectation, we make the journey home to where the *child* dwells. On the way, we will be met by friends and family who are pleased with us as we are, who remind us of successes already achieved, who will lead us to excel as persons, holy and whole.

Jesus invites us to *this* perfection; he invites us to wholeness. It is this that God seeks, to be achieved over a lifetime and yet beyond. It is blessed by grace and attained only through self-acceptance; God has already accepted us. We must touch that moment—the moment when we moved from the mind of God to God's created love. We must touch that moment because, though we were not yet capable of any willful act, we were loved. It is of no matter, necessarily, to struggle through our past, returning to that first moment of heartfelt pain and self-doubt. But it does help us to remember that although we were made from dust, our creation was truly a moment when God kissed the earth. It is this memory that enlivens us and sees us through because from the moment of our conception, through the first breath of our birth, God said, "Yes!" and affirmed our lives. We are asked by God to be as pleased with ourselves—to move in the direction of boundless love; to remember that we are the kiss of God for the earth; to stand up as the glory of God. Jesus assures us, "Your *child* will live! Your *child* will live!"

FAITH-WORD   God did not need me; God wanted me!

HEART-WORD   From the beginning I was cradled in
                     goodness. I am the cause of God's joy!

GOD'S WORD   "... I am creating [all] to be 'Joy' and my
                     people to be 'Gladness' "
                     (Is 65:18; *my translation*).

PRAYER FOR HEALING

Think back to the earliest memory of your childhood which
speaks to your drive for perfection . . .

   What comes to mind?

   How does your child feel in this memory?

   Is anyone a part of this past experience?
   As you look back, what part did they play?
   Did that person keep you from being happy or free
   as the child you would like to have been?

   What would you like to say to that person now?
   Do they respond?

Stay with this experience for awhile . . . What happens?
   Does it make you feel differently? Peaceful? Sad?

   Invite someone you trust to sit with you . . .
   Tell that person how you are feeling.
   How does she or he respond? Is it helpful? Why?

Now invite Jesus to join you, be with him awhile . . .
   Tell Jesus what you are feeling.
   Does he say or do anything? Can you respond?

   How can Jesus be with you as you continue to walk
   along the road to healing? As you strive to be yourself?

– 5 –

 From Rejection to Self-Esteem

So young, helpless—small, vulnerable.
The child reached up to touch,
but to touch whom, to touch what?
No one was there . . .
The child grew up, still reaching up
and out to touch . . .
feeling the air swirl at the turn of a skirt,
smelling the cold air of a newspaper
come home from work,
brushing against soft skin and strong bone,
but never to touch.
And as the child grew, so did a wall—
just high enough, just wide enough
to make the reaching out
and the reaching in an inch impossible.
Lord of infancy, God of childhood,
Lover of broken things—
extend your hands toward your little ones,
just an inch more,
and make the touching possible.

41

Take some time to read and ponder . . . John 9:1-41

THE PLACE OF HEALING
"I was blind, now I see" (Jn 9:25).

ILLNESS often sets up boundaries in society and highlights the isolation of human beings. In the time of Jesus, illness—disease or disability—drove a deep wedge between insider and outsider, clean and unclean. Families were torn apart. Fear separated those who were once held close by love. Illness carried the burden of guilt, as well. It was believed that those who were sick or handicapped bore the mark of sin in their flesh. Defenseless and vulnerable, they could not escape the staring eyes and wagging heads of the self-righteous—those who condemned them.

It is within this context that we are introduced to the man who was born blind. Ironically, it was the very followers of Jesus, his disciples, who put the question of sin and guilt to Jesus. "Who sinned, this man or his parents?" they asked. "Neither," Jesus answered, "he was born blind so that the works of God might be revealed in him." Yes, even this was an opportunity for grace. With spittle and dirt, Jesus offered this man the miracle of healing. Sight was born to the light of day; the blind man was able to see.

Sadly, rejection still held this man fast. Instead of joy, healing was met with hostility. After being released from a lifetime of nights, the Pharisees and his own parents struggled to clothe him with the darkness of disbelief. Fearing rejection themselves, his parents denied any knowledge of their son's healing. The Pharisees, on the other hand, were more interested in the letter of the law than in the healing of God. How was this man able to endure both the loss of parental support and religious acceptance? How was he able to stand honest and free in the face of cynicism and fear? With integrity—with the light of truth! The light of truth flooded his heart when the God of truth opened his eyes.

Healing changes us. The man in this story was not only able to commit to his healing but also to the change that it made in his life. He bore witness to the truth, despite the rejection that he met. Perhaps this is the deeper story.

There are many situations in life that can blind-side us, and when this happens we no longer walk through life but grope through it. Much like physical blindness, this blind-siding evokes fear and anxiety within, and we stumble again and again along the way. Perhaps our mother or father was the cause of this blindness—not there to help us physically or emotionally when we reached out in need; not there to hold us or catch us in their arms—unable to hear or respond to our cries. Perhaps mom or dad died when we were young, leaving us with an emptiness never truly filled. Or divorce caused a separation that never fully healed in our hearts, which were burdened by our inability to reconnect those family bonds. The *child within* continues to seek the nurturing and assurance that was missed. This *child* panics in the face of life, fearful that even adulthood will not be enough defense against an undependable and deceitful world. When this is the case, we become less curious about life and more cautious. The experience of abandonment lurks in the shadows of our every day, a menace to our inner security as unrest replaces peace.

Responsible parenting "lets go" of the child to allow maturity to take place, its rightful place. Love is at the heart of this release. When *fear* is at the root, as the parents of the man born blind remind us, relationships are strained, torn and even severed. This occurs not only between parent and child but within the child's very self. Fear is contagious. The *child within* is forever mistrusting himself or herself—fearing the inability to make sound judgments; fearing the forces that seem to be hiding beneath the surface of life; fearing the future itself.

Lacking the ability to understand such behavior, the *child* takes responsibility for the loss that has occurred. Even as adults, the *child within* cannot bear the pain and is plunged into darkness by the burden of this guilt. Anxiety becomes a traveling companion, for our *child within* is always on guard should another person or situation threaten his or her tentative hold on life.

But this blindness also prevents us from seeing who we are. Blinded to that truth, we lose sight of the value of ourselves. Jesus can walk us out of darkness into light. But to begin the journey, the *child* must move along paths that seem quite threatening and be able to admit the truth about his or her fears. That was the first step for the man who was born blind. And he persisted in the truth after he was healed, even when the Pharisees wanted him to name Jesus as a sinner, and reject the man who gifted him with sight.

From the beginning of this story God was thought to be the source of the man's blindness—God's punishment for sin. Jesus pointed out, however, that God's presence was in the healing, that God can use any situation to reveal glory. Denial of Jesus, then, would have been a sin for the healed man. Now that he could see, he was responsible for the truth.

How can this happen for us today? Our *child within* must go to Jesus and give him the fears that surround the early physical or emotional loss of parental presence, support and nurturing. We must allow Jesus to unwrap the blindness that clouds childhood eyes and lift the burden that heavies the heart of one still so young in many ways.

God never intended life as something to be survived, or even lived with stubborn independence. Neither can the past be changed. But we can develop new ways of seeing. Jesus heals the eyes of the mind, the soul and the spirit. He invites us to discover the value of ourselves as God has always known us to be. Jesus calls us out of ourselves into the light of others, too. He leads us to people who can reveal the glory of God's healing by loving us, accepting and celebrating us as God does. This is not a step back into childishness, but a step forward into the full adulthood of the children of God.

Jesus wants to reveal the *whole* truth to the *child within*. This healing vision of ourselves is gradual but, if we are faithful to the process, the God of love will shed light into our darkness. We will be able to stand strong, free from fear and open to life. The mud of the earth, that was used to heal the eyes of the blind man, is kissed by Christ for us. The *child within* can rise to meet this love. It is this love that breaks us out of the silence of darkness, for Jesus continues to speak the word of truth in us. We leave what is behind, yet we return to find what was always there—the glory revealed by God!

FAITH-WORD	The earthly chapel of my mother's womb was God's dwelling place as well.
HEART-WORD	I am also called to healing and freedom through others. I will allow someone to work a miracle in my life today.
GOD'S WORD	"Before I formed you in the womb I knew you, and before you were born I consecrated you" (Jer 1:5).

PRAYER FOR HEALING

Imagine that you are present at the beginning of time . . .

What was God saying as the first light dawned and the first life appeared?

Imagine the moment when God's thought of you became the moment of your creation . . .

Allow yourself to be born of God . . .

Rest in the arms of God . . .

What is it like to be held there?

Stay awhile . . . Allow yourself to sink into the embrace of Love . . .

Let your gaze rest on God, knowing that God first gazed on you . . .

Feel the cradling—a holding so close that Life touches life.

What words or image would best describe this experience for you?

You are the joy of God . . . feel the warmth of God's smile upon you . . .

What does God say to you by that smile?

Stay in the arms of God . . . stay within God's smile

as long as you want . . .

Return as often as you feel Jesus leading you there . . .

What may need to happen within you so that you can truly celebrate your creation with God and with those who love you?

Ask Jesus to show you the place of separation or abandonment that still needs healing.

Go there, with him, whenever and as often as you feel you are ready to face that loss . . . and receive further healing.

– 6 –

 # From Unforgiveness to Acceptance

O God,
I have a forgiving soul,
draw me to myself.
Let not the wall I feel
between spirit and desire
prevent me from making peace
with those who dwell within my past.
While I might not be able to forgive,
forgive for me.
You know I desire the homecoming
of heart and spirit,
but at this time I am incapable
of doing the good I desire to do.
O God,
I have a forgiving soul,
draw me to myself.

Take some time to read and ponder . . . Luke 15:11-32

THE PLACE OF HEALING

"Son, you are always with me, and all that is mine is
yours. But we had to celebrate and rejoice, because this
brother of yours was . . . lost and has been found" (Luke
15:31-32).

JESUS tells a story about two sons—one loyal and obedient, the other restless and shortsighted. It is worthy to notice that the father of these two men does not deny either of his sons; he accepts them as they are. He appreciates his older son while possessing an openness that frees his younger son to learn the lessons of life on his own.

In this parable, we hear so much of what the younger son did with his inheritance, how he recklessly squandered what he had that, by the time he returns home to the open arms of his father, we can't help but stand with the older son and complain: *unfair!* "All these years I have been working like a slave for you, and I have never disobeyed your command; yet you have never given me even a young goat so that I might celebrate with my friends" (Lk 15:29). This son feels neglected, frustrated, insulted that loyalty and obedience were undone (in his mind) by reckless, careless living. Worst of all, his Jewish father welcomed home a son who had become a Gentile, and treated that son with the love to which outsiders were not entitled.

Yes, the younger son did squander his father's inheritance, but the older son squandered his father's generosity.

Perhaps this sort of sibling rivalry has been played out in our own lives. When this happens, we begin to live a life centered in comparisons and, too often, fight the battles of envy. The *child within* has never resolved the anger and resentment of earlier "injustices" and carries that painful burden into adult life. This *child within* seeks to attain value and self-worth through the diminishment of others, ever wanting to balance the scale of dutiful behavior with the rewards of attention and recognition. Ever envious, this *child* only relates to others through competition. There is a driving need to be noticed, to be justified, even to be rewarded for a moral life. Eventually, our *child within* learns that life does not always work that way. As individual and unique as human behavior can be, so the consequences of our actions do not always obtain our desired or even reasonable response.

Anger follows the *child* through life in the form of power plays and self-righteous behavior. Our unforgiveness of the past lurks just beneath the surface of daily life, ready to strike out and strike down anyone who challenges our tentative hold on self-esteem. Envy eats away at the *child within*. Life cannot be enjoyed. Rather it is destroyed by the need to be number one, come out on top, get attention at all costs. Anger also lashes out at those in authority who are expected to respond reasonably to the hardworking, dutiful, untiring older son within us. "After all I did for you!" we complain. "How could you pass me by? How could you miss all my time and effort?" Disillusionment destroys, even further, our striving for maturity and self-worth.

Little by little, nothing and no one is right anymore. Nothing and no one can be trusted. Complaints become the chorus of our days. The growth of our *child within* has been stymied by the hopelessness of our demands. What can save us from ourselves? What can help us move from feelings of betrayal to trust? What can lead us down the road of life with peace of heart, yet with integrity? What will enable us to discover the value of who we are, what has been and what can be?—ACCEPTANCE will.

Acceptance does not mean giving in. That would only increase our anger. Acceptance does not mean excusing. That would deny reality. Acceptance is the reaching out for new life, true life. It is the willingness to move on, no longer dependent upon the actions or attention of others. No longer dependent upon "pay back" or equal consideration. The key phrase is: no longer dependent. It is preceded by awareness. We come to our senses. We finally realize the damage we do to ourselves and to others. Unforgiveness comes with a price. In wanting others to pay for their behavior, in wanting others to have less recognition than ourselves, we become poor. Unforgiveness prevents us from entering the joy of others. Like the older son who could not join the celebration of his brother's return, we are left outside. Why? Because we choose to enter through a door we ourselves have locked by our resentment. God says to the older son within us: "But he's your brother . . . she's your sister. Can't I be generous? Worthiness is not the issue here. Love is. Will you really allow your need for competition to keep us apart . . . to keep you from the family of humankind?"

It is difficult to forgive—to accept another as brother or sister, to accept them as they are; to accept the circumstances of our lives because they simply were; to let go of previously thought of rights, the feeling of being owed better treatment. Our *child within* wants to heal, if truth be told. We really do want to accept life on its own terms. We want to stop the struggle that time and again does not resolve—the battles that cannot be won, the resentments that wear us down and weaken the resilience of our spirit.

Are some people beyond the limits of our mercy? Are we beyond the limits of God's? Can we claim for ourselves rightness and integrity while denying others the same? God is not fragile or frightened by the fury of our *child within*. Neither does God expect us to deny or excuse reality. When we become aware of how we have suffered by not accepting life and moving on, we can begin to heal. But forgiveness does not come at once. In fact, we may need to ask God to forgive that person until we catch up to the spirit of acceptance we seek. The insight and desire to accept and move on recurs throughout our lives. But if the effects of our envy and competition, our sibling rivalry, last a lifetime, so does the presence of grace. We must not lose heart. God, who began this good work in us, will bring it to completion.

Once we want to be healed, once we want to accept and move on, God will not give up on us. The desire is the beginning of our healing. Grudges, hurts, hostility, envy will leave the heart of our *child within* slowly but surely. Eventually, this will lead us beyond acceptance to forgiveness and the freedom for which we long. As this happens, we will understand the words of the father to his older son, " . . . you are always with me, and all that is mine is yours." The struggle for attention will subside and that will be enough for us. To our surprise it will be enough.

FAITH-WORD	God, who begins the work of healing within me, will bring it to completion.
HEART-WORD	I am enough. I do not need to have an advantage in order to have value.
GOD'S WORD	"Lord, you know everything; you know I love you" (Jn 21:17).

PRAYER FOR HEALING

Call to mind a place of peace. Rest there.

> Invite several friends to join you. Those who accept you as you are.
>
> Do they say anything as they sit with you?
>
> Ask them to stay with you as you continue this prayer.

As you prepare to receive the grace God wants to give you . . .

> Breathe in and out slowly and deeply.
>
> Ask Jesus to send the spirit of acceptance with each breath.
>
> Let God's Spirit fill you.

Relax and open your hands.

> Ask Jesus to share with you his willingness to accept life and others as they are.
>
> Let your open hands be a symbol of surrender, a giving up of any struggles that may be going on in your life.

Can you remember the person you first began to struggle with for attention?

> Invite them to join you, remembering that you are already surrounded by those who love you.
>
> If this is difficult, ask Jesus to bring him or her in to you and to remain with you in this prayer.
>
> How else might Jesus strengthen and encourage you?
>
> Ask him for that gift.

Speak to the person of your memory.

> Tell him or her what you felt at that time.
>
> Again, remember that you are surrounded by those who love you.

Does that person reply? What does he or she say to you?

> Is this helpful?
>
> Continue in conversation, inviting Jesus and perhaps one of your loved ones to join you.

As you continue, become aware of your breathing.

> Breathe in the Spirit of God . . . the spirit of acceptance.
>
> Breathe out a prayer of thanks.

Become aware of your open hands.

> Consciously release any tension, any fears or anxiety you may feel. Do this as you breathe out your prayer of thanks.

As you conclude this time of prayer, thank Jesus and your loved ones for their presence.

Ask the person you brought to prayer to leave a gift of peace with you as you let him or her go.

Ask Jesus to bless your friends who were with you in prayer and all those who struggle as you have.

Promise them your prayers for healing as well.

– 7 –

 From Nameless Dread
to Knowing Peace

Help me, O God,
to lift fear from my shoulders
and throw it off the edges of the world,
defying the gravity that lays it upon me
time and time again.
Let it fall into its own orbit,
perhaps encircling me and this earth,
but never again crashing down upon me—
crushing me to a pulp
of palpitating, shattered forevers.
I pray for all those who, like me,
awaken with nebulous foreboding.
Be with us—help us to cast out fear
by love, by you, by grace.
Lift us from ourselves on days like this,
out of the murky depths of this unknown threat,
into the light that shines above and around us . . .
within us.
Let us see your face.

Take some time to read and ponder . . . Mark 9:14-27

THE PLACE OF HEALING

Immediately the father of the child cried out, "I believe; help my unbelief!" (Mk 9:24).

A S Jesus descends the mountain with Peter, James and John to rejoin the other disciples, he is greeted by a scene of unrest. He finds a crowd, particularly some scribes, arguing with his disciples. There is a sense of chaos—the clashing of opinions, a babble of words. How meaningful that this would come to reflect the inner world of confusion in the boy possessed, the boy Jesus would soon be asked to heal.

Jesus comes upon this scene and asks what is going on. He is answered: "Teacher, I have brought you my son." Then the father of the boy goes on to describe the terrors, disabilities and dangers that his son has had to endure from childhood. He speaks of the boy's muteness. He tells Jesus about convulsions that throw his son into fire and water, that cause him to foam at the mouth, grind his teeth. And finally, his son's frail body seems cast in stone each time the boy becomes rigid with seizures.

Yes, this father asks for pity from Jesus but, above all else, help. How his heart must have ached with each thrashing round of his child. Had his own body turned to stone, each time his son seized with convulsions? Had he come to fear the warmth of fire for their winter home? The necessity of its heat for food? Or the nearness of a lake for refreshing coolness? After all, rather than providing well-being, these had become dangers for his son. Words must have failed to describe his own pain over so many years—voiceless, the cries of his heart.

Here is a weary man, grown old beyond his years from worry, fear, attentive love . . . parental love. Here is a man who sees Jesus as truly a God-send. Perhaps it is from Jesus that he drew the strength to breathe forth those words—"if you can do anything, have pity on us and help us."

What follows is a most wonderful dialogue between this father and Jesus, ending with a proclamation of faith that speaks a very human truth: faith can be affirmed, even while mixed with doubt. Jesus tells the boy's father, "Everything is possible for one who has faith!" At once the father of the boy cried out, "I have faith. Help my lack of faith!" That was all that Jesus needed because faith lives in the quiet corner of desire. From more than pity, Jesus spoke from compassion and commanded the unclean spirit to leave the man's son and never to enter him again. With cries and terrible convulsions, the spirit left the boy in total exhaustion—his body still and at last at peace. The gospel tells us that Jesus took him by the hand and he was able to stand up.

Today, we recognize the disease of epilepsy as we read this gospel story; but these symptoms can sometimes be the experience of our *child within.* A nameless, free-floating anxiety that we cannot describe, and for which we have no words, can assail the spirit of the *child within.* It is an apprehensive expectation that clouds the mind, and casts a shadow upon our day-to-day living. Worry is difficult to control and, like the boy possessed, our *child within* goes thrashing through the hours of the day, fearing the fire of distress that seems to burn the heart out of all we do.

For the *child within,* this pervasive and ongoing apprehension prevents freedom of movement, as if we were imprisoned within our very selves. Restlessness, which strains against those bars, easily fatigues. This helplessness feeds hopelessness. The *child within* is left weary after each seizure of nameless dread. Yet this very helplessness and hopelessness can draw breath from the power of Jesus, who loosened tongues, stilled fears and set captives free. With trust that help is there for the asking and hope opens the door to freedom, our *child within* can cry out, "I have faith. Help my lack of faith!"

Even today, all that Jesus asks for is a living faith. Not necessarily unwavering, fearless belief, but faith like the father had in this gospel—one that can be professed and expressed while doubt and fear still walk alongside the human heart. Like a tiny seed that has living within its roots full growth, this faith in Jesus will break through the foreboding darkness to shine in the light of healing peace. Jesus will cast light into the corners of the heart of our *child within,* and reveal a way of living that we have longed to know—a way of living that will release peace and usher the *child* into freedom.

We may need someone to care for us along the way, to guide and keep us safe . . . much like this father did for his son. Someone who can help us read the words and decipher the pictures of our inner struggle. Someone who can enable the *child within* to name the worries and fears that have tormented the heart, burned the spirit, drowned all hope. Someone in whom we can trust until we can trust ourselves.

Peace will come. Peace will come when faith and inner work walk hand in hand. Jesus will be there, not just at the beginning of this journey but through to its end. His healing grace will give power to the *child within* to take his hand, stand up and walk on with firmness and freedom.

FAITH-WORD	To know myself and the world as a loving gift is to know the joy of God.
HEART-WORD	I was born into the God of peace. When I no longer pursue my fears, I will find myself at home there, once again.
GOD'S WORD	". . . indeed God is not far from any of us, since it is in God that we live, and move, and exist" (Acts 17:27-28; *my translation*).

PRAYER FOR HEALING

Have you awakened with an unsettled feeling?

Uncomfortable and anxious, as if the pieces of your life will not touch together?

Gently take one of those moments, or mornings, into your hands . . . What is its name?

Invite that experience to feel safe, surrounded by your care and desire to be at peace.

Where does this loving presence lead you?

Allow that special part of you to tell you its needs . . . What does it say? How can you respond?

God is always with us . . .

God leads us, at times . . . God carries us, at times . . .

When have you felt this to be so?

What was it like for you?

God sends Jesus into the lives of people who are in need.

Invite Jesus to be with you now . . .

Ask him to help you know that you are held safe by his love . . .

Ask him to help you realize that you hold peace in your heart, not just toward others, but for yourself.

Does he speak in your heart?
What does Jesus say?

Be with Jesus as he embraces the peace that is you . . .
Can you help him? How?

What must yet happen for you, so that you can know the peace of Jesus within and around you?

Ask Jesus . . . then trust that he will show you the way.

Is there anyone who might walk with you on this road to healing?
Invite him or her to be with you and Jesus now . . .

How does he/she help and support you?
Can this continue to happen? How?

Thank Jesus for this person in your life.

– 8 –

 From Depression to Hope

Holy Simplicity, holy God—
I wake in anxious wonder
and find the unraveling of my day.
I race
to weave the loose ends,
knotting them
so that the flow of energy
might not be wasted.
Holy Simplicity, holy God—
Grace my weaving with receiving.
Draw me
to the sanctuary of my soul,
and let me linger there,
waiting on the still, small voice
of Spirit-wisdom
to speak my heart's desires.
Then my day
will be born of you.
And night will find me resting easy—
borne by you.

Take some time to read and ponder . . . Mark 5:21-43

THE PLACE OF HEALING
"Little girl, get up!" (Mk 5:41).

THERE was much dissension about Jesus among the leaders of the temple, but now the barriers of politics fade away in the face of human need. Jairus, president of the synagogue, was at wits' end with the prospect of losing his daughter; without question, his child's life must come first! Jairus seeks out Jesus, for he finds hope in the power of the Healer. Desperate, he falls at the feet of Jesus and begs for his daughter's life, "Come and lay your hands on her, so that she may be made well and live" (Mk 5:23). Moved with compassion, Jesus goes with him.

The crowd followed—pressing, pushing on all sides. Then what happened startled even Jesus. Someone touched his cloak. Not that the crowd hadn't, but this was different—this touch was the touch of faith. He could feel the healing power go out from him. "Who touched me?" he asked (Mk 5:31). It was a woman, but she was trembling with the realization that she was cured and could not speak. Like Jairus, she, too, had been desperate, hemorrhaging for twelve years. The life force flowing out of her had left her weak and drained of hope. Now, finally, she found healing. The healing flowed from Jesus, stemmed the flood of death that rushed from her body and dried the tears of despair that threatened her spirit.

Jesus searched the crowd. Every cure took something from him especially when the energy of his healing was accepted and embraced. He wanted to find the person who received his blessing. It was important to Jesus to see a face, to look into eyes and to affirm the faith that gifted that touch. It wasn't magic. Turning to God is itself a gift of God; yet God, through Jesus, is much disposed to healing. Finally the woman came forward—"Daughter," Jesus said to her, "your faith has made you well; go in peace, and be healed . . ." (Mk 5:34). We hear few words from this woman; simply put, "she told him the whole truth," but to this day we remember her courage and her faith.

No sooner did Jesus set out again than word came of the child's death. Jesus told Jairus not to be afraid, but to have faith. It is remarkable that in the face of death Jairus still held fast to his belief in Jesus; yet he did. Arriving at his home, he and Jesus saw that the ritual of mourning had already begun—family and neighbors weeping, wailing, crying out. Yet this did not disturb Jesus, "The child is not dead but sleeping," he said to them (Mk 5:39). Then, walking past their ridicule and disbelief, Jesus went to the child, took her hand and said, "Little girl, get up!" (Mk 5:41). Faith defies even death! Instantly, she arose and walked around. This gift of life transformed even family and friends. Depression, which entered their hearts like a thief robbing them of peace, was lifted by the touch of Jesus.

The *child within* can appear to be dead as well—asleep with depression, the sleep of the living dead. Whether it affects a child of twelve or an adult suffering for twelve years, depression lays a heavy blanket over courage and hope dissolves into despair. Limbs are heavy, the mind is clouded, the home of the heart feels empty. Weariness becomes a daily burden until it is as if one's body, itself, weeps day and night.

In the face of all this fly the words of Jesus—"Do not fear, only believe" (Mk 5:36). But with depression, the question is always HOW? How do I wake up from this sleep of depression? How can I think beyond the moment when the future looms with such foreboding? How can the weeping cease when laughter has become a memory? How will I ever walk again when effort, itself, is paralyzed? The answer, as always, is Jesus.

Jesus is present in the very experience of all that happens to us. He is present with us; he does not stand and watch us from afar. Jesus knows the despair, fears and apprehensions of our *child within*. He knows the emptiness of our hearts and the weariness of our bodies. Jesus does not shake his head in sadness and walk away. Jesus is there, always there, ready to rekindle our experience of joy and awaken us to life. But the *child within* must go to that place of pain and seek the grace of God. It may feel as difficult as pushing our way through a crowd, but Jesus is closer than arm's reach, longing to touch and be touched.

We may feel drained of hope but our life-force is the resurrection of Jesus Christ. This fills us with courage—a courage we will discover only by being courageous. This courage pushes the *child within* through the limits set by despair. It pushes us beyond our fears to new hope. Perhaps our *child within* may not have an advocate like Jairus; then we must parent ourselves. We must go to Jesus on behalf of our *child within,* summon the strength that we fear is lost forever, find it, and fling it at our doubts. This is faith! Faith can cost us, but this coin is cast in healing. Jesus wants to hold our hearts as he did the hand of Jairus's daughter. Jesus desires to lift us from depression and ransom the theft of our *child within*.

Today we cannot make physical contact with our healer, Jesus Christ, but his power is still available to us. Jesus offers us one another to touch and be touched, to trust and be trusted. If we but lift a hand, we will meet his in the help we can receive—faith heals through human touch, as well. This touch cradles our *child within* until we, too, can respond to the words of Jesus, "Daughter (Son) . . . go in peace, and be healed . . . ."

FAITH-WORD   God is not discouraged with me even when I am discouraged with myself.

HEART-WORD   From the moment I was conceived, God said: "I believe in you!"

GOD'S WORD   "I will not forget you. See, I have inscribed you on the palms of my hands" (Is 49:15-16).

PRAYER FOR HEALING

Find a place outdoors (even in your mind's eye) where you can be alone . . .

Allow the sun to shine on your face . . .

Feel the warmth . . .

Let it spread over you then through you . . . taking time to experience, again and again, its warmth and brightness . . .

Let this be Jesus—let the rays of the sun be the light of Christ . . .

This light spreads over you . . . through you . . . around you . . .

What is this like?

How does it feel?

What comes to mind?

Is it something you can share with Jesus?

Something you can bring to prayer?

Rest, once again, in the healing warmth of Jesus . . .

Is there something still cold within you?

Something within the shadows which has not yet met that healing light?

Can you name that place or space?

Invite whatever is still in darkness to meet the healing light of Jesus.

Hold it out toward the light . . . Toward Jesus . . .
Jesus within you and around you.

Keep it there and allow his brightness to lighten and brighten it . . .

Let the warmth of his healing soften any edges of this night, calming the fears within and around you. Stay here awhile.

Do you feel a change?
Can you put this feeling into words?

Arms of hope placed you on this earth . . .

Can you play at the feet of God? Of Jesus?

How would you do that today?

As you live and work this day, be aware of God's look of love . . .

How/where might you experience it?

– 9 –

 From Fear to Freedom

Lord Jesus,
wash away my iniquities,
cleanse me from my sins.
Cleanse me from the sins
of mothers and fathers,
strangers and neighbors,
that have been visited upon the children.
—that have been visited upon me.

Take some time to read and ponder . . . John 6:1-13

THE PLACE OF HEALING
Here is a small boy with five barley loaves and two fish (Jn 6:9).

EVEN before Jesus' time on earth, children were looked upon as a blessing—a gift from God (Gn 4:1, 33:5); a crown of the aged (Prv 17:6); the heritage of God (Ps 127:3-5). But Jesus intensifies their significance by using children as examples in his teaching about the kingdom, humility and greatness. "Children" was the term he used to address his disciples (Mk 10:24); the word he connected with conversion

(Mt 18:3); the characters in some of his parables (Mt 11:16-17). One day, Jesus even used a young boy's lunch to feed a crowd of five thousand.

Yes, in the context of a Eucharistic account in the gospel according to John, we find a child at center stage. Jesus is concerned for the needs of the crowd that had followed him across the sea of Galilee. "Where are we to buy bread for these people to eat?" he asked Philip (Jn 6:5). Philip's response was concern about the prohibitive cost of feeding such a large crowd. Andrew saw a young boy with a few rolls and fish, but knew that would never be enough. Jesus surprises them all by taking the boy's food, blessing it and giving thanks to God. Then, what was once a meager sustenance for one becomes a banquet of bread and fish for thousands.

As we look back on this gospel account, we know that Jesus is pointing to a bread that will give us daily nourishment and more—eternal life—for Jesus is this Bread of Life. But we can also learn something from this young boy. An almost instinctive generosity is apparent. When the disciples approached him with their need, we do not read any reticence on the child's part—no reluctance to share the little he had. We do not even read that his parents had to intervene. He was asked and he gave. This boy did not question how his few loaves and fish would satisfy the hunger of the crowd. He trusted the disciples that this lunch of his would somehow do.

Children believe almost everything. Children believe almost anything is possible. They are blessed with the gift of imagination and are easily mesmerized by the simplest things in their ever-growing world of experience. Most importantly, children place full confidence in those who lead them, and full trust in promises made. Sadly, though, the openness, spontaneity, generosity and trust of some children is betrayed. Their openness is violated; their spontaneity, abused; their generosity, pillaged by greed; their trust, victimized by aggression.

These innocent children feel responsible for the crimes committed against body, mind and spirit. They withdraw in fear that the truth of their experience will be revealed. They see themselves as ugly—ugly from the inside out. Even at a young age, they know that something is wrong, inappropriate, painful about this experience. Children know it for what it is—an act of violence—even though they may be too young to give it its name. And too young to save themselves, they continue on helpless, until or if someone rescues them.

When Jesus asked for the boy's bread and fish, he was also asking for the treasured presence of that child. Jesus did not use people. He respected them, loved them, knew them as his brothers and sisters. Jesus held children, not to smother them or impress the people who followed him. Jesus held and embraced children because he knew others would not always value them. Jesus knew, then and now, the crimes of the heart that twist real love into lust. Yes, the child grows into adulthood, but the *child within* continues to be a child. Only now, the joy of childhood has turned to tears; freedom is replaced by fear; and trust is securely locked away. The *child within* suffers—weighed down by the burden of blameless guilt.

Jesus longs to restore the image of the *child within*. He longs to restore it to its divine countenance—the image of God who is truth, beauty and goodness. Jesus weeps with our tears, shivers in our fears, stands with us behind locked doors. But Jesus can and will dry those tears, quiet our fears and open the door to inner freedom. Healing begins with the grace to grieve, but this is a difficult grace for which to ask. It means facing our fears as the tears continue to flow. It means discovering the truth, long hidden under years of betrayal. It means reaching out for help, until someone reaches in. It means *allowing* someone to reach in with healing love. It means reclaiming the gifts of childhood, now as an adult—capable of making choices, naming experiences, placing responsibility where it belongs. It means seeking the face of God within, trusting that the divine will be found.

When we are this *child*, we must take heart by taking the hand of Jesus. We must ask him to lead us to the persons, places and words that will unlock our truth, restore our sense of beauty and regain our freedom. The journey may be long; the road complex with twists and turns, but we are assured: "When you search for me, you will find me; if you seek me with all your heart" (Jer 29:13). We must pray for one another to take heart . . . as we take the hand of Jesus, our Christ.

FAITH-WORD	My broken world is held in the hands of my healing God.
HEART-WORD	Faith has placed me in the womb of God. From there, I pass through the door of God's healing promise.
GOD'S WORD	"Stand at the crossroads, and look, and ask for the ancient paths, where the good way lies; and walk in it, and find rest for your souls" (Jer 6:16).

PRAYER FOR HEALING

You may want to begin this meditation by calling to your mind's presence, someone you love and trust.

Gently invite that person into your prayer, when and if you feel you need a loving presence . . .

Find a special place—a sacred space—and there, rest your mind, heart and body—that sacred place is you.

Listen to the sounds around you . . .

Listen to the sounds within you . . .

What do you hear?

Wait on a word of joy . . . peace . . . gentleness . . .

Repeat that word within you . . . stay with its feeling.

What is this like for you?

Does it lead you to another word . . . and another?

Invite Jesus to be with you as each word of God's love and peace holds your body, heart and spirit in a healing embrace.

Remain there as long as you wish.

Does anyone join you and Jesus in this prayer?

Is it someone you know and love?

Is it someone you did not expect?

Are you able to welcome him or her?

If you can, tell that person how he or she may help you . . .

Ask Jesus to lead you and that person to the healing you ask for in this prayer.

Follow Jesus wherever he leads . . . to a feeling, an image . . . you are safe there with him.

Talk to Jesus about this . . .

Ask him to help you know yourself as the gift that God intended you to be to the world . . .

Or just rest in the safety of his presence.

Return to this experience in prayer as often as you feel it is helpful.

– 10 –

 From Grasping to Grace

God of freedom,
you call me to be still and to listen.
You call me to taste the touch of grace.
But it is a hard place for me to be, Lord Jesus—
this place of letting go.
Your promise of peace unsettles me,
yet never cease your call
to know as I am known.
Haunt me with wordless sounds.
Draw me to dynamic stillness, again and again.
Keep encircling me, grasping me,
capturing me with a hold so strong
that I dare not let go.
Make me taste the touch of grace.
Make me taste the touch of grace.

Take some time to read and ponder . . . Luke 7:11-17

THE PLACE OF HEALING
And Jesus gave him to his mother (Lk 7:15).

B E it expected or unexpected, the death of a loved one robs us, and that loss seems so final. Our own lives are fractured, and a corner of our hearts is ripped away.

Death brought tears to the eyes of Jesus, too. He was no stranger to this land of loss. In this gospel story, Jesus came upon a widow in the heart of her grief—the funeral of her only son was in progress. For a widow in a patriarchal society, this meant that she had no bridge of recourse or advocacy. Her fate was grim. Seeing her grief, Jesus was moved to compassion. He understood her loss and the prospects of her future. He walked over to her and gently said, "Do not weep" (Lk 7:13). Jesus did not intend to shield her from reality or to abort her mourning. Jesus sought to soften the edge of her grief, a grief that stabbed her heart and cut her from the fabric of Jewish society.

Jesus preached liberation from all that would harm or destroy us. In him, death would receive a final blow and bow before God—powerless; but now he would unshackle one of its prisoners. Jesus stepped into the widow's world and walked her past the laws of ritual impurity by touching her son's dead body. He said simply, "Young man, I say to you, rise!" (Lk 7:14). At those words, the widow's son sat up and began to speak. To this day, we are warmed by the tenderness of Jesus as "he gave him to his mother."

Through and in Jesus, God visits us. Whatever our condition, whatever the circumstance, God draws near; Jesus is held captive by the needs of the human heart. For the widow in this story, death did not end with the pain of emptiness; death became an encounter with the caring and compassionate Christ. Life was restored to both mother and son. A future opened out and the promise of salvation was acclaimed.

This bond of mother to son and son to mother was sealed in love, but cemented in survival. There are times, though, when bonding between people—family or friends—arises from quite another need. The *child within* fears that, alone, he/she will not survive. Filled with this fear, our *child within* cries out for connection, a connection that was not satisfied earlier in life—a time when, as an infant, he/she was most vulnerable and most in need. This cry reaches the heart of another, but because it is anchored in fear, our *child within* unwittingly twists the bond of connection, cutting off the lifeline of that relationship. This fear reaches out and lays hold of whoever might be near—grasping, clutching, yet never embracing, for embracing allows for a healthy separation. Yet separation is unthinkable to this *child within.*

Emerson once said, "My friends come to me unsought." Freedom is the hallmark of friendship. Freedom is the hallmark of all healthy relationships. Our lives do depend upon one another, but not as a crutch supporting a weakened limb. Friendship is more like a garden whose charm is enhanced by the variety of its flowers and the beauty of their array. Sadly, for this *child within* to stand apart and enjoy the beauty of another is quite impossible. Instead, anxiety from the fear of being alone sends the *child* racing through the garden plucking, if not trampling, its flowers.

What will ever assure this *child within?* Who would ever be able to stand near, yet withstand the grasp of this *child*—a grasp so fierce that it drains the life out of loving relationships? The "who" is Jesus. The "what" is grace.

After the resurrection, when Mary recognized Jesus in the garden outside the tomb, Jesus said to her, "Do not hold on to me" (Jn 20:17). Maybe those words have something to teach our *child within*. Our lives achieve a healthy dependence with Jesus. He is the Divine Gardener who knows about weakened limbs, the need for light, protection, and good earth. Jesus supports our growth by planting us in holy ground—the life of God. It is from there that we can send forth roots that nourish the inner self. Jesus strengthens and encourages us to make our way toward the light of each new day. He knows, that when we surface with our individual personalities and gifts, the earth will be lavished with a beauty unique to humankind—a blessing for one another. Jesus cherishes the fruit of our creation.

The Son of God has warmed the earth with a presence that will never leave us. Our lives can depend upon him for he is dependable. Jesus invites the *child within* to stand free and to unwrap the cloak of fear that hides our true self. He stands beside us as a companion, yet he invites us to an intimacy that is beyond our wildest dream—Jesus lives within us and promises to remain with us all days and in all ways!

As he did for the widow of Nain, Jesus will restore the *child within* to life anew. With compassionate mercy, Jesus restores us to ourselves. The grace of God visits us again and again. This grace gifts the *child within* with freedom, so that we can celebrate relationships and enrich the soil of one another's lives.

FAITH-WORD	Healing comes from surrender, not from control.
HEART-WORD	I know my longing for God, but do I also know God's longing for me?
GOD'S WORD	"I have loved you with an everlasting love; therefore I have continued my faithfulness to you" (Jer 31:3).

PRAYER FOR HEALING

Ask Jesus to bring you to a place of deep longing in your life . . .

Even if you cannot name that place, trust him to lead you there . . .

Feel the breath of God sweep over that place in your heart, caressing your deepest longing . . . embracing it.

What does this breath of God touch or awaken within you? Sit with this awareness and hold it gently for awhile.

Now walk through the doors of your earliest memory . . .

Is there something that still must be unlocked for you? Ask Jesus to go to that door . . .

Does he wish to open it for you? With you?

Is there something that blocks the way?

Is it a person? Or a feeling?

Ask Jesus what you should do.

Often, within our heart of hearts, there is a place only Jesus can enter . . . What is that place for you?

Invite Jesus there . . . be with him . . . stay awhile . . .

Does he do or say anything to you about this place?

All of our longings speak to us of our longing for God . . .

Can you find that longing for God?

Invite God to cast out your fears.

Ask Jesus how it might set you free . . . How you might set another free.

Jesus longs to bless you with the freedom and trust of his love—a love that respects as well as cherishes you . . .
A love that respects and cherishes others.

Of what must you let go in order to be free?

Of what must you let go in order to know that love in your life?

Ask Jesus to be with you and to help you to that freedom and to the inner trust in your goodness.

A Meditation of Joy

Child of Light—
Countenance of God
reflected within and about.
Promise of hope
renewed and resounding
in a gentle heart—
The Lord is with you!
Abundant waters flow . . .
Creator, Word and Spirit
leave the mark of God
on your young flesh—
enlightening . . . lifting . . .
searing your soul
in pursuit of unending love—
relentless in desire for union
with you . . .
Child of Light!

Prayer Services and Rituals

(for private use or during retreats, as time and circumstances allow)

– 1 –

♟ Gathering ♟

Preparation

Table with articles and items reminiscent of childhood.

(baby picture, baby shoes, First Communion prayer book, picture of parents, brothers and sisters, etc.)

Sharing

Invite those present to add something to the table of memories.

Each person receives a nametag with first name and its meaning/translation.

(I recommend *Name That Baby!* by Jane Bradshaw and published by Broadman & Holman, Nashville, TN, 1998. It is detailed and comprehensive, providing 5,000 names, their meaning and biblical reference.)

Invite each person to introduce themselves with their name and its translation/biblical meaning. Ask each to share a story about their name, their godparents or baptism event.

After sharing, invite all to carry the "meaning" of their names throughout your time together. And to ask God to make them aware of the particular grace to which their name and reflections may lead them.

Closing Prayer Our Father . . .My Child (by Anita M. Constance, S.C.)

Beginning with "Our Father," two sides of prayer circle alternate as they pray:

Our Father	MY CHILD
who are in heaven,	WHO ARE ON EARTH,

Hallowed be your name.

BLESSED IS THE NAME I CALLED YOU FROM YOUR BIRTH.

Your kingdom come.

BRING THE KINGDOM ABOUT, MY CHILD.

Your will be done on earth as it is in heaven.

LET ME BE GOD IN YOUR HEART AS I AM IN ALL MY CREATION.

Give us this day our daily bread,

TODAY YOU WILL HAVE ALL THAT YOU NEED.

and forgive us our trespasses as we forgive those who trespass against us.

FORGIVE THOSE WHO HAVE HURT YOU FOR MY SON SAID: "BLESSED ARE THE MERCI-FUL. . . ."

And lead us not into temptation, but deliver us from evil.

I WILL LEAD YOU ON THE RIGHT ROAD, THOUGH YOU MAY KNOW IT NOT . . . YOU HAVE MY WORD: DEATH IS NO MORE, "ITS HOUSE LIES SHATTERED! "

For yours is the kingdom, the power and the glory forever and ever. Amen.

COME, SIT DOWN AND BREAK BREAD AT OUR TABLE, AND YOU WILL BE FILLED WITH THE POWER OF THE SPIRIT. . . . ALL THAT WE HAVE IS YOURS—FOREVER AND FOR-EVER AND FOREVER. YOU HAVE MY WORD, MY LOVE, MY PROMISE. I HAVE CARVED YOU ON THE PALM OF MY HAND.

– 2 –

 By Name I Have Called You

Opening Song   By Name I Have Called You

(text and music: Carey Landry ©1980, NALR)

Reading 1   Proverbs 22:1

A good name is more desirable than great riches,
And high esteem, than gold and silver.

(pause for reflection)

Reading 2   Luke 10:17-20

(pause for reflection)

Reading 3   Ephesians 3:12-16

(pause for reflection)

Response to Readings   Psalm 139:1-18, 23-24

(pray together)

Chorus of Names

During this time each person will speak the name of persons for whom they wish to pray, or to mention the name of someone who has been very significant to their life's journey. In a spirit of prayer, these will be spoken spontaneously so as to become a chorus of names presented to our loving and compassionate God.

Reflection *(can be read aloud by one or two persons)*

I am born of God...a daughter, a son of the Trinity—created, redeemed and healed. From the beginning of time, this God said, "Yes" to me. . .

———

Before I was, you knew me, O God.
You gazed on me with love
and rocked me in arms of hope.
Your wisdom saw beyond my present.
Your faith in me beheld the beauty.
You saw my greater truth and brought
into being creation, as you knew it.
What happened mattered not to you,
as much as your belief in me . . .
Image and likeness would endure
the test of brokenness and time.
Believing does such things.
So today and every day,
I make my act of faith in you—
for long ago, with whispered breath,
you credoed me to life.

(from *Night Vision: Praying through Change* by Anita M. Constance, S.C.)

Closing Song   Saints of God in Glory

(play recording)   (Bernadette Farrell, OCP)

– 3 –

Morning Praise

Be still within and without.

Breathe in the peace of Christ, breathe out any thoughts which disturb you.

Let yourself be fully present to this moment.

Song Hello, My God
   (play recording) (Monica Brown, Emmaus Productions)

Opening Prayer Loving God, we gather in the morning light to listen to your Word in the many ways it comes to us each day…in the grace of each morning. Teach us to listen as Mary did— attentively—so she could hear an angel's soft whispers, her cousin Elizabeth's excited greeting, her baby's first cry, and most of all her God in the depths of her heart. Help us to be open as Mary was as we begin this day.

Reading 1 John 1:1-5, 9-12

Reading 2 (from *The Mother of Christ* by Caryll Houselander)

Many rejoiced, not first of all because she was to be the mother of God, not first of all in the sweetness of having a child of her own, but because her child was coming into the world to be light, humility, gentleness, justice, for the healing of the wounds of pride, because he, who now lived in her was the world's life, and his love would prevail from generation to generation.

Mary gave birth not only to the Christ in history, but to the Christ in all of us, she gave her good simple life to be the substance of his life in us.

Reflection

Take some moments of quiet time to reflect on the following:

Who first gave birth to God in your life?

Who introduced you to God?

Who taught you to pray?

(On paper provided, write the name(s) of the person(s) you recall. Approach the table one by one, say the name(s) aloud and place your paper in the basket on the table. We now bring these people to be with us on our journey to new life.)

Closing Prayer

Gracious God, give me the grace of today...
the grace of the present moment,
the grace to be present to the moment.
Free me from my wanderings and wonderings.
Empty my cluttered mind, releasing the confusion
of my private tower of Babel.
Loosen my grip on life so that life may grasp me,
and take me where it will.
Open my heart when I bar its door,
preventing others from entering in.
Let me walk in the footsteps of ordinary time
to enjoy the dance of each day.

Let there always be a light in my eyes
to mirror your presence in my soul.
A smile on my lips to welcome strangers
and laugh at the clowning in this greatest show
called earth.
—a spirit of forgiveness to heal the brokenness
that I share with others.

—the grace of celebration to remind me
that you are God.
—and a sense of peace, your peace,
to carry me through the rhythm of TODAY.

(from *Night Vision: Praying through Change*
by Anita M. Constance, S.C.)

– 4 –

Closing Prayer

Opening Song   Brother Jesus   (Carey Landry, NALR)

Reading 1   Matthew 10:13-15

Response   *(introduction read by one person)*

I have often prayed the creed of my faith, but now I wonder
what God might say in response to my belief. In a way, I think
that God believes, too . . . And God says:

———

I believe in you—
the reflection of my glory, co-creator of the kingdom
and child of my love, my blessed one:
conceived by grace—my word made flesh...
who suffers because of the poverty
within your human beauty, and the frailty
of a world that stands on tiptoe anticipation—
groaning and longing for the birth of new life.

I believe in you—
called to share the death and darkness
of the grain of wheat . . . who at times experiences
the depths, only to know the height,
the breath and life of resurrection—
at home with me, sharing the joy of my Son,
who heals and brings peace in his loving embrace.

You have lived in the presence
of the breath of life, whose hushed whispers
you have welcomed into the corners of your heart.

You dwell with sisters and brothers beyond
the boundaries of your home.
Many have prayed for you—far beyond your imagination—
enabling you to know forgiveness and to offer mercy.
Now, go and live because...
I believe in you!   (from *Night Vision: Praying through Change*
                                    by Anita M. Constance, S.C.)

Name Blessing   *(Bookmarks/or other remembrance have been prepared with each person's name and its referenced Bible verse. Each person is called to the center of the prayer circle. The leader presents each person to the group by given name, followed by its meaning. Then bookmark is given to each person.)*

Leader This is _____, _____ and beloved of God.

All   May God continue to give you abundant blessings.

(Once all have been called and presented, continue with the following prayer.)

Prayer of Thanks

Lord, thank you for each moment,
          for the shared moment,
                    the listening,
                              the unguarded word,
          for the fragile openness,
                    the ready smile,
                              the accepted difference,
          for my passionate heart
                    and the trust rooting in me.
Stretch me
          to grow with whatever comes as a gift
                    and to praise you in it.

Lord, thank you for each moment,
    for the charged moment,
        the confrontation,
        the accurate demand,
    for the hard decision,
        the breathless gamble,
        the unexpected growing,
    for my intense heart
        and the truth expanding in me.
Excite me
    to be open to whatever comes as a gift
        and to praise you in it.

Lord, thank you for each moment
for the holy moment,
    the music,
        the child's eyes,
    for the sunlight,
        the touch,
        the tears,
    for the trembling pleasure,
        the unutterable beauty,
        the breathing,
    for the life and love and heart in me, aware,
        and the wholeness spreading in me.

Touch me
    through whatever comes as a gift
        that I may be graceful
            and praise you in it all.

(from *Guerrillas of Grace* by Ted Loder)

Ritual and Closing

Each person is invited to take a small ceramic baby shoe from the basket that was placed at the table of memories before the prayer began. Each person receives this remembrance as the song *God Beyond All Names* by Bernadette Farrell (available from OCP) is played in the background.

(special acknowledgment to Julie Scanlan, S.C. for the above prayer services)

In addition, one may also excerpt and reflect upon for further meditation:

Suggestions for Further Reading

Beckman, Richard J. *Praying for Wholeness and Healing.* Minneapolis: Augsburg Books, 1995.

Bergan, J.S. and M. Schwan. *Praying with Ignatius Loyola.* Winona, MN: Saint Mary's Press, 1997.

Berry, Karen. *Beyond Broken Dreams.* Cincinnati: St. Anthony Messenger Press, 1984.

Bloomfield, Harold and Philip Goldberg. *Making Peace with God.* New York: Tarcher/Putnam, 2003.

Bondi, Roberta C. *In Ordinary Time: Healing the Wounds of the Heart.* Nashville: Abingdon Press, 1996.

Borg, Marcus, J. *Meeting Jesus Again for the First Time.* San Francisco: HarperSanFrancisco, 1994.

Bradshaw, John. *Healing the Shame That Binds You.* Deerfield Beach, FL: Health Communications, 1988.

———. *Creating Love: The Next Stage of Growth.* New York: Bantam, 1992.

———. *Homecoming: Reclaiming and Championing Your Inner Child.* New York: Bantam, 1992.

Brewi, Janice and Anne Brennan. *Celebrate Mid-Life: Jungian Archetypes and Mid-life Spirituality.* New York: Crossroad, 1988.

Campbell, Peter R. and Edwin McMahon. *Bio-Spirituality: Focusing as a Way to Grow.* Illinois: Loyola University Press, 1985.

Cheston, Sharon E. *As You and the Abused Person Journey Together.* New York/Mahwah: Paulist Press, 1996.

Constance, Anita M. *Night Vision: Praying through Change.* New York/Mahwah: Paulist Press, 1998.

de Mello, Anthony. *Sadhana: A Way to God.* St. Louis, Missouri: The Institute of Jesuit Sources, 1978.

Dickinson, Emily. *Selected Poems and Letters of Emily Dickinson.* Garden City, NY: Doubleday/Anchor, 1959.

Downs, Alan. *The Half-Empty Heart: A Supportive Guide to Breaking Free from Chronic Discontent.* New York: St. Martin's Press, 2003.

Ford, Debbie. *The Secret of the Shadow: The Power of Owning Your Whole Story.* San Francisco: HarperSanFrancisco, 2002.

Gould, Roger L. "The Phases of Adult Life: A Study in Developmental Psychology." American Journal of Psychiatry, 129 (1972) 33-43.

—————. *Transformation: Growth in Adult Life.* New York: Simon & Schuster, 1978.

Jung, Carl. *Modern Man in Search of a Soul.* New York: Harcourt Brace, 1939.

—————. *Man and His Symbols.* New York: Doubleday, 1964.

Keating, Thomas. *The Human Condition: Contemplation and Transformation.* New York/Mahwah: Paulist Press, 1999.

Linn, Dennis, Sheila Fabricant and Matthew Linn. *Good Goats: Healing Our Image of God.* New York/Mahwah: Paulist Press, 1994.

Linn, Matthew and Dennis Linn. *Healing of Memories.* New York: Paulist Press, 1974.

Merton, Thomas. *New Seeds of Contemplation.* New York: New Directions, 1961.

Metz, Barbara and John Burchill. *The Enneagram and Prayer: Discovering Our True Selves Before God.* Denville, NJ: Dimension Books, 1987.

Miller, John A. *Your Golden Shadow: Discovering and Fulfilling Your Undeveloped Self.* San Francisco: Harper & Row, 1989.

Morneau, Robert F. *Mantras from a Poet: Jessica Powers.* Kansas City, MO: Sheed and Ward, 1991.

————. *A Retreat with Jessica Powers.* Cincinnati, OH: St. Anthony Messenger Press, 1995.

Norwich, Julian. *Revelations of Divine Love* (Trans. M.L. del Mastro). New York: Doubleday, 1977.

Nouwen, Henri J.M. *On Mourning and Dancing.* The New Oxford Review, June 1992.

————. *The Inner Voice of Love: A Journey through Anguish to Freedom.* New York: Doubleday, 1996.

Palmer, Parker J. *The Active Life: A Spirituality of Work, Creativity, and Caring.* San Francisco: Jossey-Bass Publishers, 1990.

Pastor, Marion. *Anger and Forgiveness: An Approach That Works.* Berkeley, CA: Jennis Press, 1990.

Powers, Jessica. *The House at Rest.* Carmelite Monastery, Meadowbrook Rd. Pewaukee, WI, 1984.

Rahner, Karl. *The Great Church Year.* New York: Crossroad, 1993.

Ripple, Paula. *Growing Strong at Broken Places.* Notre Dame, IN: Ave Maria Press, 1986.

Rolheiser, Ronald. *The Holy Longing.* New York: Doubleday, 1999.

Rupp, Joyce. *Praying Our Goodbyes.* Notre Dame, IN: Ave Maria Press, 1988.

———. *May I Have This Dance?* Notre Dame, IN: Ave Maria Press, 1992.

———. *Little Pieces of Light.* New York/Mahwah: Paulist Press, 1994.

———. *Dear Heart, Come Home.* New York: Crossroad, 1996.

———. *The Cup of Our Life: A Guide for Spiritual Growth.* Notre Dame, IN: Ave Maria Press, 1997.

Sanford, John A., *Dreams and Healing.* New York: Paulist Press, 1978.

———. *Dreams: God's Forgotten Language.* New York: Crossroad, 1984.

Savary, Louis M. and Patricia H. Berne, New York/Mahwah, NJ: Paulist Press, 1988.

———. and Strephon Kaplan Williams. *Dreams and Spiritual Growth: A Judeo-Christian Way of Dreamwork.* New York/Mahwah: Paulist Press, 1984.

Sheehy, Gail. *Passages: Predictable Crises of Adult Life.* New York: Dutton, 1976.

Shlemon, Barbara Leahy, *Healing the Hidden Self.* Notre Dame, IN: Ave Maria Press, 1982.

Siegfried, Regina and Robert Morneau, eds. *Selected Poetry of Jessica Powers.* Kansas City: Sheed & Ward, 1989.

Singer, June. *Boundaries of the Soul.* Garden City, New York: Anchor Books, 1973.

Vennard, June E. *Praying with Body and Soul.* Minneapolis: Augsburg Fortress, 1998.

Welch, John. *Spiritual Pilgrims: Carl Jung and Teresa of Avila.* New York/Mahwah: Paulist Press, 1982.

Whitehead, Evelyn Eaton and James D. *Christian Life Patterns: The Psychological Challenges and Religious Invitations of Adult Life.* New York: Crossroad, 1995.

Wicks, Robert J. *Seeking Perspective: Weaving Spirituality and Psychology in Search of Clarity.* New York/Mahwah: Paulist Press, 1991.

————. *Touching the Holy: Ordinariness, Self-Esteem and Friendship.* Notre Dame, IN: Ave Maria Press, 1992.

————. *After 50: Spiritually Embracing Your Own Wisdom Years.* New York/Mahwah: Paulist Press, 1997.

————. *Living a Gentle, Passionate Life.* New York/Mahwah: Paulist Press, 1998.

————. *Simple Changes: Quietly Overcoming Barriers to Personal and Professional Growth.* Allen, TX: Thomas More Publishing, 2000.

Wiederkehr, Macrina. *Seasons of Your Heart.* San Francisco: HarperSanFrancisco, 1991.

Additional Titles Published by Resurrection Press, a Catholic Book Publishing Imprint

For a free catalog call 1-800-892-6657
www.catholicbookpublishing.com